Mike Patrick's

Superstars of Speedway

Oxford Publishing Co.

ISBN 0-86093-271-0

Origination by: Colthouse Repro Ltd.,
Bournemouth

Printed in Great Britain by:
Butler & Tanner Ltd., Frome and London

Published by:
Oxford Publishing Company,
Link House,
West Street,
POOLE, Dorset.

Introduction

Well, here it is folks — my third book devoted entirely to the exciting sport of speedway.

This publication is a little bit special to me, as it marks my tenth anniversary as a professional photographer within the sport. This time, I have decided to cut out all those boring words that are usually found in books, to make way for lots and lots of pictures. In fact, the only words written within its pages are the captions to the photographs.

It has taken an entire winter close season to put together, searching and researching through more than 80,000 photographs. Eventually, I selected about 750 shots that I wanted to use, but, alas, I only had room for a third of that amount. It was no easy task making the final selection, but I sincerely hope that you find the resulting book pleasing.

Most of the pictures were taken during the late 1970s and early 1980s, but there are some earlier shots which I hope will jog a few memories.

I personally regard speedway as the most exciting of all motor cycling sports. It is also a sport rich in colourful personalities and entertainers. I wish I could have included photographs of every single one of them, but there was insufficient room. However, I hope the pictures that I have chosen will convey what a wonderful sport speedway is.

It is terrific to be able to combine two great loves, photography and speedway, and earn a crust at the same time. It is hard work but, as I always say, it's better than working for a living. I hope you enjoy this book as much as I have enjoyed these past ten years.

The LIONS of England

Plate 1: Taking a short breather between races at White City.

Kenny Carter

Plate 2: Kenny rides inside his biggest rival, Bruce Penhall.

Plate 3: Leading Lance King, Joe Owen and Merve Janke at Cradley.

Plate 4: Elbow to elbow action alongside Reg Wilson at Halifax.

◄ *Plate 5:* After the controversial incident with Bruce Penhall at Los Angeles in 1982, the angry Yorkshireman is escorted from the track by one of the L.A. 'heavies'.

Peter Collins

Plate 6: His greatest moment . . . World Champion in Poland, 1976. Peter is joined on the rostrum by Malcolm Simmons (2nd) and Phil Crump (3rd).

Plate 7: Abensberg, 1973, and Peter heads Gregori Chylnovski and Tommy Jansson during the European Final.

Plate 8: In full flight during the World Long Track Final, 1982.

Plate 10: The caption to this shot can be left to your own imagination. I'm not going to risk it! ▶

Plate 9: Attempting to ride speedway and grass track at the same time during the 1979 World Final in Poland.

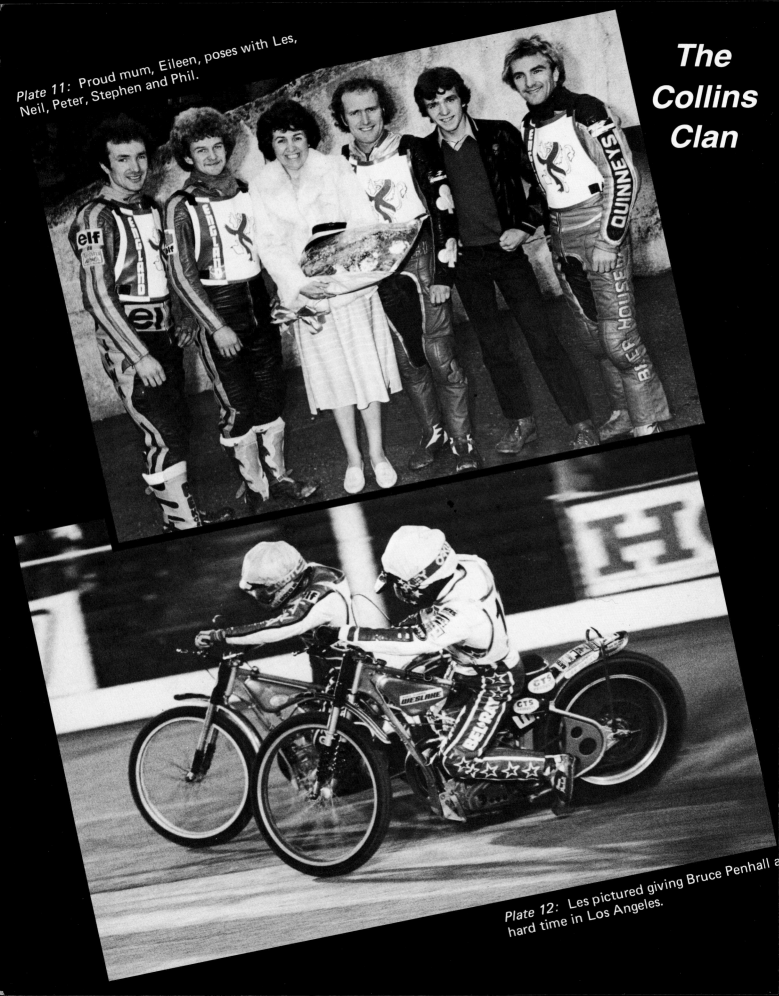

The Collins Clan

Plate 11: Proud mum, Eileen, poses with Les, Neil, Peter, Stephen and Phil.

Plate 12: Les pictured giving Bruce Penhall a hard time in Los Angeles.

Plate 13: Phil heading Simon Wigg in Long Track action.

Plate 14: Les, No. 2 in the world in 1982.

Plate 15: Thrilling the fans at Belle Vue, Les pulls a wheelie during Peter's testimonial.

Dave Jessup

◄ *Plate 16 (top left):* Leading Mike Lee and Ole Olsen in Poland, 1979.

◄ *Plate 17 (bottom left):* Wembley's unluckiest man. Another long walk back to the pits after being dogged by motor troubles during the 1981 World Final.

◄ *Plate 18 (bottom right):* Wearing the colours of the famous Wembley Lions, D.J. makes his way around Wimbledon in this early shot.

Plate 19 (right): Between heats at Leicester.

Plate 20 (below): Flat out action as Dave rides inside Bobby Schwartz and Malcolm Simmons at Swindon.

Plate 24 (right top): No doubt about it! The young lady points out the winner of the 'Knobbly Knees' contest during a SWAPA versus Stars of Speedway soccer match.

Plate 25 (bottom right): Superb team riding at Cradley, as Chris and Larry Kosta keep Dave Perks at bay.

Plate 23: Flashback to 1975 as Mighty Mort peers over his bars at full throttle.

Plate 21 (above): Warming up his bike prior to a meeting in Vojens.

Plate 22 (right): Leading Alan Grahame out of the second bend at Cradley.

Chris Morton

Michael Lee

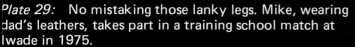

Plate 26 (left):   Mike powers to his World Title under the Gothenburg floodlights.

Plate 27:   An anxious moment as Michael lifts ahead of Penhall and John Titman.

Plate 28:   1974 — a cheeky faced 15 year old faces the camera at the King's Lynn press day.

Plate 29:   No mistaking those lanky legs. Mike, wearing dad's leathers, takes part in a training school match at Iwade in 1975.

John Davis

Plate 30: The joy of victory. John celebrates leading Reading to the top of the league in 1980.

Plate 31: The sorrow of defeat. A lonely man in the Coventry pits as elimination from the World Championships is imminent.

Plate 32: John leads John Louis, Ashley Pullen and Steve Baker at Halifax.

Plate 33: Still idolized by many at Oxford, Gordon heads Ed Strangeland and John Dews during a league match against Wimbledon.

Plate 34: April 1973 saw a change of hair colour which didn't last for long.

Plate 35: Gordon heads Ole Olsen to the chequered flag in West Germany.

Gordon Kennett

The Grahame Brothers   Steve Bastabl

Plate 36:   Alan and Andy, on parade at Leicester.

Plate 38:   The 1981 British Champion speculates before a race.

Plate 37:   The Brothers Grahame team riding during an England versus Denmark test match.

Plate 39: 1983 . . . A new English star emerges, Simon Wigg.

Simon Wigg

Malcolm Simmons

Plate 40: Malc on the inside, and Mike Lohmann, make a Jerzy Rembas sandwich at Rodenbach in 1978.

YANKIE DOODLE DANDIES

Bruce Penhall

Plate 43: As good on one wheel as he is on two.

Plate 44: All action at King's Lynn, as Penhall is chased by Mick McKeon, Bruce Cribb and Chris Morton.

Plate 41: The tears flow as the new 1981 World Champion is greeted, in the Wembley pits, by sister-in-law Keri and girlfriend Josie.

Plate 42: Penhall moves alongside Carter just seconds before that controversial crash in Los Angeles in 1982.

Plate 45

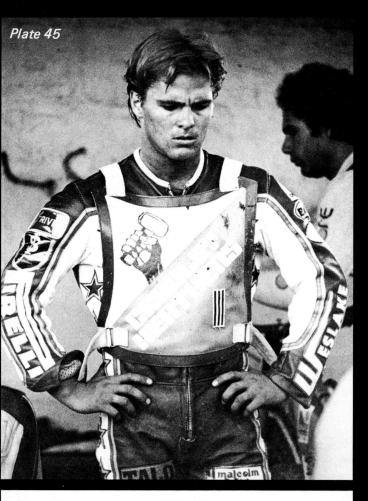

Plate 46

Plate 47

Juicy Brucie

—in the Mood

Plate 48

Plate 49

Plate 50

Plate 51

Plate 52

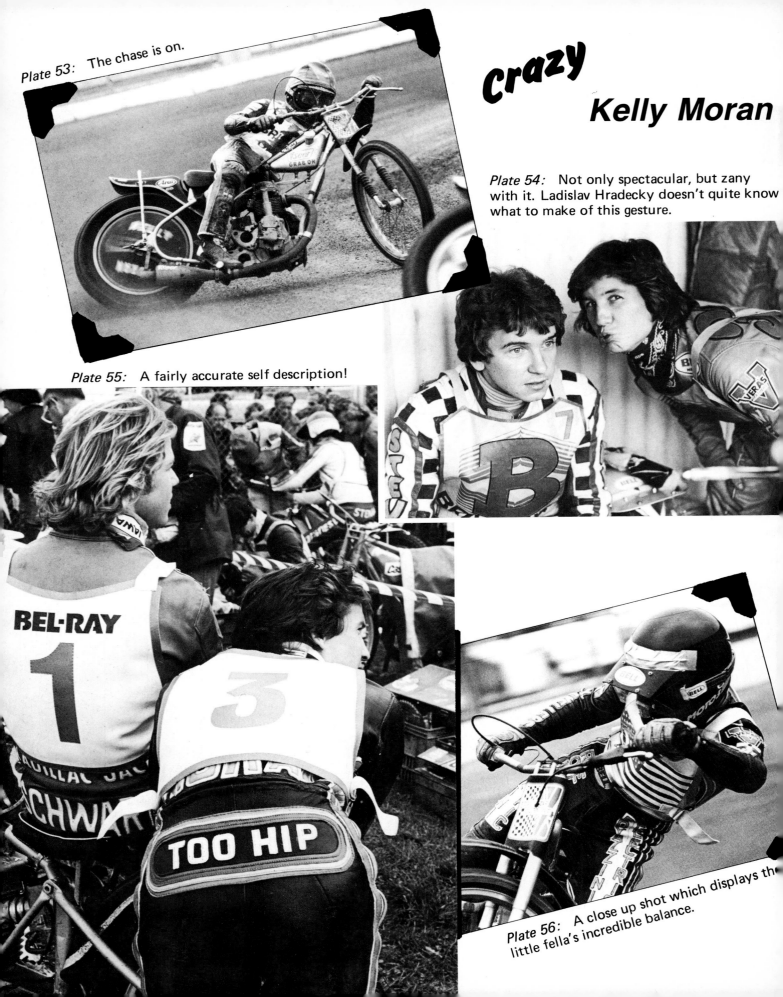

Plate 53: The chase is on.

crazy
Kelly Moran

Plate 54: Not only spectacular, but zany with it. Ladislav Hradecky doesn't quite know what to make of this gesture.

Plate 55: A fairly accurate self description!

BEL-RAY
1

3

TOO HIP

Plate 56: A close up shot which displays th little fella's incredible balance.

Plate 57 (above): Kelly's lightweight frame hangs on to his machine at Coventry.

Plate 58 (right): 'Nervous, who me?'

Plate 59 (below): Leading Peter Collins, Jan Andersson and Edward Jancarz at White City.

Shawn Moran

Plate 63 (top right): In typical action as the little Yank lead Jan Andersson.

Plate 64 (below right): 'That's my boy' — Bobby Schwartz congratulates Shawn on his match winning ride at Swindon.

Plate 61 (above): Shawn in thoughtful mood.

Plate 60 (left): 'Who's this guy in the Rupert Bear trousers' — Shawn and Kelly.

Plate 62 (below): Lifting off alongside Bruce Penhall.

Plate 66 (top): An emotional moment for Bobby a he injects his own enthusiasm into Penhall during th 1982 World Team Final, which the USA went on to win.

Plate 65 (top left): Checking his bike in the Reading pits.

Plate 67 (below): Long Tracking in Denmark

Bobby Schwartz

Plate 68 (above): 'Boogaloo' gives a wave to his pals in the pits at Wembley Arena.

Plate 69 (right): Deep in thought, on parade at Swindon.

Plate 70 (below): Leading Jessup and Morton during a test match at Poole.

Dennis Sigalos

Plate 72: Concentration at the tapes during a test match at Poole.

◄ Plate 71: A relaxed pose from the popular Yank prior to a meeting at Rijskijk, Holland.

Plate 73: In close combat with Billy Sanders at White City

Plate 74 (above): One of the great showmen of speedway, Siggy, shows the fans that he's no novice when it comes to skateboarding.

Plate 75: Entertaining again, this time on one wheel.

Plate 76 (right): A contrast in mental preparation. Siggy sits deep in thought, whilst Penhall hides away beneath his cap at Vojens in 1981.

Scott Autrey

Plate 77: There was a time when these three gents were the only Americans in the British League. Sumner McKnight, who looks half asleep, Rick Woods and a hippie-looking Scott Autrey

Plate 78: Autrey just holds on to the lead ahead of Peter Collins and Roger Abel.

Plate 79: At the tapes, Autrey lines up against the man who replaced him at Swindon, Steve Bastable.

Plate 80: Pictured with his good friend Steve Gresham — a man who seems to spend more time on crutches than on his bike.

Plate 81: Not the best way to drink while wearing a full face helmet.

Plate 83: Spectacular action as John throws his bike into the bend.

Plate 82: Relaxing in the Swindon pits.

John Cook

Ron Preston

Plate 84: A real nice guy, but plagued by injuries since coming to Britain.

Steve Gresham

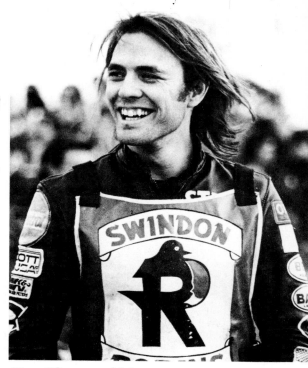

Plate 85: Living up to his wild image,
Steve loses his wheel at Reading . . .

Plate 86: . . . which seems to amuse
young Steve.

Plate 87: A great future has been predicted for this youngster.

Lance King

THE DASHING DANES

Ole Olsen

Plate 88: The man who has performed miracles for Danish speedway celebrates his team's success after victory at King's Lynn.

Plate 89: Not such a happy moment this time for the Danes, as they watch their World Team title slip away at White City in 1982.

Plate 91 (right): Olsen in complete control.

Plate 90: 'C'mon Ole, you must have some cash on you, after all, it is your turn to buy the lollies.'

Plate 92: Still in control, Ole gets a nudge from Reidar Eide during a World Pairs meeting at Poole in 1973.

Plate 93: Can you believe this? Erik as he looked in 1979.

Erik Gunderson

Plate 94: This is more like the chirpy chappie that we all know and love. Even he seems amused by the picture on the left.

Plate 95: 'Think I'll stick to speedway — it's safer.' Erik tries his hand at BMX.

Plate 96: Flat out action.

Plate 97: Two thrill makers side by side — Erik and Chris Morton.

Hans Nielsen

Plate 98 (top left):   Nielsen leads out of the fourth bend at White City, while Penhall, Mauger and Autrey kick up the dust at the rear.

Plate 99 (bottom right):   More than competent at indoor speedway, Hans leaves the gate at Wembley outside Chris Morton.

Plate 100 (bottom left):   No, it's not Penhall with a perm. Hans had his leathers stolen from his car the night before, so Bruce obliged with a pair of his for the White City practice.

Plate 101 (right):   Keeping cool at the Costa Del White City.

Plate 102 (below):   Too close for comfort. Sigalos gets a nudge from the Dane at King's Lynn.

Tommy Knudsen

Plate 103: A champion of the future. Tommy acknowledges his fans at Vojens.

Plate 104: Riding indoors at the Ahoy Stadium in Rotterdam.

Plate 105: Finishing third in his first World Final, he leads Jan Andersson at Wembley.

Plate 106 (above):   Leading Lee, Sanders and Mauger at White City.

Plate 107 (below left):   Mike Lohmann looks awe-struck at the sight of the Finn's fashionable attire.

Plate 108 (below right):   'Peek-a-boo, I can see you.' Warming his bike at Coventry.

Finn Thomsen

Bo Petersen

Plate 109: Relaxing on parade at Reading.

Plate 110: An anxious moment for Bo as he lifts ahead of Penhall and Kel. Moran at Vetlanda, Sweden.

Plate 111: A young man with great prospects. Benny heads Sigalos and Knudsen at Coventry.

◀ Plate 112: Young 'Witch' on his home track.

Plate 113: Benny keeps a keen eye open at the Wembley practice.

The Flying Finn

Plate 114: Kai is very competent on the indoor circuits.

Plate 115: Keeping cool under the midday sun in Los Angeles.

Kai Niemi

There are not many Finns on the scene at the moment, but Kai Niemi has made steady progress over the last few years and has still to reach his peak.

Plate 116: Taking the outside line against Nielsen and Gundersen at Vetlanda.

(Right): Splendid wheelie performed by Kelly Moran at King's Lynn.

WHOOPS!

Plate 117 (above): Five riders bite the dust in a junior race at Costa Mesa.

Plate 118 (right): Vaclav Verner gets the old heave ho from Bob Coles at Mildenhall.

Plate 119 (below): Ivan Mauger and Alan Grahame hit the concrete at Wembley Arena.

Plate 120: Not recommended. Mike Caroline practices his wall of death act around the Oxford safety fence.

Plate 121: Bob Coles, David Ashby and Ian Clark in a right old pickle at Milton Keynes.

Plate 122: Another fine mess . . . Joe Hughes is the rider going east whilst Trevor Jones chooses a westerly direction at Canterbury.

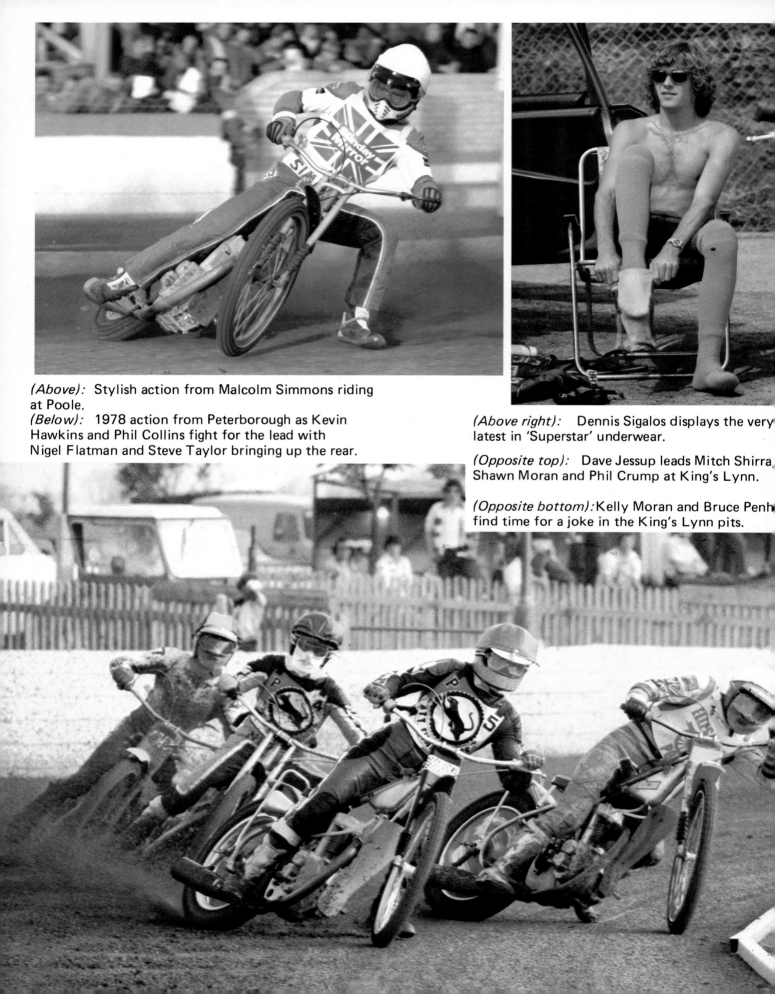

(Above): Stylish action from Malcolm Simmons riding at Poole.

(Below): 1978 action from Peterborough as Kevin Hawkins and Phil Collins fight for the lead with Nigel Flatman and Steve Taylor bringing up the rear.

(Above right): Dennis Sigalos displays the very latest in 'Superstar' underwear.

(Opposite top): Dave Jessup leads Mitch Shirra, Shawn Moran and Phil Crump at King's Lynn.

(Opposite bottom): Kelly Moran and Bruce Penh find time for a joke in the King's Lynn pits.

CRASH!

Plates 123 to 128: During a close race with Ole Olsen and Soren Karlsson at Coventry, Martin Ashby bails out and has a lucky escape after hitting the pit gate.

late 129 to 134: John Barker changes course in mid-corner and heads
or the fence. He was lucky not to take Mike Fullerton and Les Rumsey with
im.

BANG!

(Previous page): Phil Crump heads Andy and Alan Grahame at White City.

Plates 135 to 138: Doug Wyer tangles with his machine at White City, and although Peter Collins manages to lay down, he was unable to avoid him.

Plates 139 to 143: Ian Jeffercoate pictured getting into all sorts of trouble at Oxford. I bet he couldn't sit down for a week after that one!

(Above): 1973. Surprise winner in Poland, Jerzy Szczakiel is joined on the rostrum by Ivan Mauger and Zenon Plech.

(Above right): Michael Lee's moment of glory in Gothenburg, 1980.

(Below): 1974. Gothenburg again, as Anders Michanek takes the World crown with runners up Ivan Mauger and Soren Sjosten.

Above): Peter Collins celebrates, with wife Angela, after the 1976 Final in Poland.

Above right): Ivan Mauger makes speedway history as he takes his sixth crown in Poland, 1979.

Below left): Miss World 1978, Mary Stavens, with Ole Olsen as he takes his third crown. Runners up are Scott Autrey and Gordon Kennett.

Below right): Top of the World for the second time and immediate retirement for Bruce Penhall — Los Angeles 1982.

WALLOP!

Plate 144: Dave Jessup had a lucky escape after this fall at White City.

Plate 145: John Davis demolished the fence and the lamp standard at Poole in 1978. It's a wonder they ever signed him after that!

Plate 146: Carl (Spear) Askew lances Rob Mounce after having already caused havoc with Ivan Blacka and John Hack in the background.

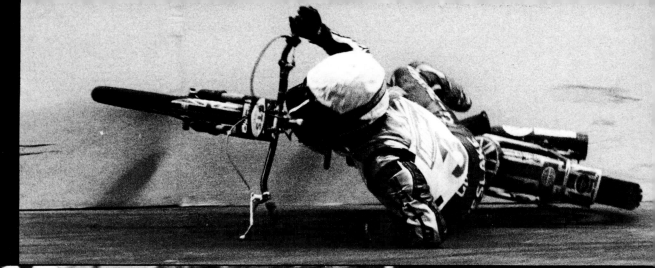

Plate 147: Indoor speedway seems to drive Peter Collins up the wall.

Plate 148: Rolf Gramstad takes a [na]sty tumble at Leicester.

Plate 149: As any ice racer [k]nows, not a happy position to be [i]n. The late Zdenek Kudrna is the [r]ider heading for Joe Hughes.

(Above): Flat out action from Kenny Carter at Coventry.

(Below): John Davis and Michael Lee discuss tactics in the Wimbledon pits.

(Above): Dave Jessup showing concentration at the tapes.

(Below): The exciting style of Shawn Moran entering the first bend at Cradley.

SIZZLING SWEDES

Anders Michanek

Plate 150: Gothenburg in 1974, and wife Margarita joins Anders on the victory parade.

Plate 151: Steve Bastable gets into trouble behind Mich at King's Lynn

Plate 152: Demonstrating his superb control on the concrete, Andersson thrilled the crowds with this great celebration 'wheelie'.

Jan Andersson

Plate 153: The unofficial World Indoor Champion receives his trophy at Wembley in 1982.

Plate 154: Reading. Jet-propulsion from the tapes at

Plate 155 (top): Jan and brother Bjorn keep a watchful eye on the opposition at the 1981 Wembley practice.

Plate 156 (bottom): Indoors again, and the undisputed master leads Joe Owen, Preben Eriksen and Malcolm Simmons.

Richard Hellsen

Plate 158 (top right): In the pits at Swindon

Plate 157 (top left): Team riding with Richard Greer at Oxford in 1975.

Plate 159 (below): Hellsen looks for partner Mike Lee, who is busy keeping John Davis at bay.

ANZAC ACES

New Zealand

Ivan Mauger

Plate 160: Happiness is Kiwi-shaped. Mum and wife, Raye, share Ivan's joy after winning his fifth World Title in Gothenburg.

Plate 161: In perfect control on the tight Birmingham circuit.

Plate 164 (right): Ivan presents his one time protegee, Ole Olsen with the Ricard trophy.

Plate 165 (top right): Revealed the secret of Ivan's eternal youth

Plate 166 (bottom right): Andy Grahame, giving Ivan a tough race at Birmingham.

Plate 162 (left): 'Hey Sprouts, you sure that you and Ole are "ju good friends?".'

Plate 163: Leading Chris Morto during the 1976 World Final in Poland.

THE TONY BRIGGS FILE

Plate 167: 1972, and young Tony looks as if he's more interested in his copy of the *Beano* than the tactics discussed by his dad Barry, Bjorn Knutsson and Ronnie Moore.

Plate 168: Tony poses with brother Gary and idol, Ole Olsen, in 1973.

Plate 169: Pedal power, albeit as a passenger. Tony watches dad practice at Wimbledon. Now I know where my Mercedes insignia got to.

Plate 170: Father and son pose for the press in London, at the Tony Briggs/Faberge launch.

Plate 171: After a serious accident in 1981, young Briggo was left out in the cold while his fellow riders practiced at the start of the 1982 season.

Plate 172: Challenging Scott Autrey at Reading.

Plate 173:   One for the girls.

Plates 174 to 178:   Like father — like son. Young Briggo experienced quite a few sticky situations, just like dad in his early years.

Larry Ross

Plate 179:   A talented Kiwi
who has still to reach his peak.

Plate 180:   Splendid action
as Larry gives Les Collins a run
for his money.

Mitch Shirra

Plate 182 (above): Chatting in the Wimbledon pits with good friend Gary Guglielmi.

Plate 181 (left): A fiery little Kiwi, pictured here with father, Tom, in 1974 while riding illegally under age.

Plate 183 (below): Mitch rides inside Zenon Plech at Coventry.

Phil Crump

Australia

Plate 184 (top left): Crumpie in typical action while the Bristol Bulldogs were alive.

Plate 185 (top right): Relaxing at a practice session.

Plate 186 (below): A Crump sandwich, as Phil leaves the tapes between John Davis and Peter Collins.

Billy Sanders

Plate 187: Flat out action as Billy The Kid is chased around the Brummie raceway by Joe Owen.

Plate 188: Keeping an eye on the proceedings in Poland.

Phil Herne

Plate 189 (top left):   'The Kid' being nursed by Dave Gooderham.

Plate 190 (top right):   In flat out action at Reading.

Plate 191:   Leading team mate Neil Collins at Reading.

John Titman

Plate 192: Sanders gives a word of advice to John before a vital race at White City.

Plate 193: White City again, and a hectic chase to the flag inside Malcolm Simmons.

CONTINENTAL CRACKERS

Plate 196 (below): Long Track Action from Denmark. There is no doubt that the Germans rule in this particular sport. Egon Muller (15) and Alois Wiesbock (3) head Anders Michanek (18) and Georg Gilgenreiner (14) to the first bend.

West Germany

◄ *Plate 194 (top left):* Mr Nice Guy, Karl Maier, is crowned World Long Track Champion, 1982.

◄ *Plate 195 (top right):* Karli greets one of his younger fans at Birmingham.

Czechoslovakia

Plate 197 (top): Jiri Stancl hits a spot of bother. Other riders are the late Denny Pyeatt, Phil Collins and Andy Reid.

Plate 198 (left): One for the family album. Antonin Kasper gets a shot of his talented young son, Toni.

Plate 199 (below): Ales Dryml being chased by Bruce Penhall.

DO, DO, DO YA REMEMBER

Plate 202: . . . those super Swedes, Tommy Jansson and Christer Lofqvist, both, sadly, no longer with us?

Plate 201 (top right): . . . the voice (!) of Reg Luckhurs

Plate 200 (top left): . . . when Les Rumsey had hair — and lots of it?

Plate 203: . . . the 1973 World Champion, Jerzy Szczakiel, seen here attempting the limbo dance under the Oxford safety fence?

Plate 204: . . . when Eastbourne used to win trophies?

Plate 205 (top left): . . . when John Davis had black hair?

Plate 206 (top right): . . . 'I'll kill Mike Patrick for printing that picture?.'

Plate 207 (above): . . . Wembley in 1973, when the result of the World Test series rested on a match race between Collins and Michanek? The Englishman went flying and Michanek was excluded. The stadium erupted as England was announced the winner.

Plate 208: . . . when a team of zany Scots defected south of the border?

Plate 209: . . . Egon Muller thrilling the crowds at Chasewater in 1977?

Plate 210: . . . a cheekie chappie called Joe Owen *(right)*, appearing on the scene. Here he links up with Chris Roynon and brother Tom in Barrow's colours.

A Funny Thing Happened...

Plate 211: 'How would one of you good looking chicks like to co-star in my next film?'

◄ Plate 214: 'Are you sure you didn't put itching powder in my leathers, Bob?'

Plate 215: 'Don't you reckon that's the smartest team picture you've ever seen, Neil?'

Plate 213: 'The things that some riders get up to in their spare time amazes me.'

Plate 218: 'Ooh, Ivan, I can't bear to watch!'

Plate 220: 'Get yourself a pair of pants like that son, and maybe, one day, you'll be Captain of England.'

Plate 222: 'Is that what they call leg-trailing, dad?'

Plate 223: 'Just checking to make sure everything's still in its right place.'

A Funny Thing Happened cont...

Plate 224: 'But Gregori, there must be a shop that sells Russian zippers somewhere in Wolverhampton.'

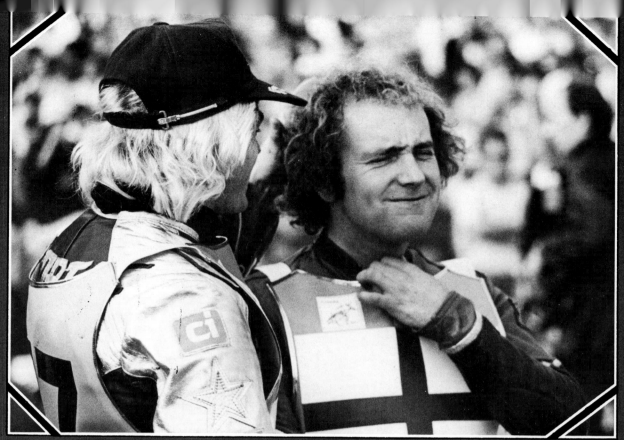

Plate 227: Either the Poles make their race-jackets too big or the Brits make their riders too small. P.C. feeling some discomfort . . .

Plate 228: . . . while Dave Jessup remedies the situation with a pair of scissors.

Plate 229: 'We're a couple of swells.' Erik Gundersen and Phil Collins having a slapstick time.